Let Your Worries Go

JESSICA HURLEY
ILLUSTRATIONS BY PADDY BRUCE

 St. Martin's Press

Library of Congress Cataloging-in-Publication Data

Hurley, Jessica, 1970–
Let Your Worries Go / Jessica Hurley ; illustrations by Paddy Bruce. – 1st ed.
p. cm.

ISBN 0-312-26531-X

1. Stress management. 2. Worry dolls--Guatemala. I. Title.
RA 785 .H87 2001
155.9"042--dc21   00-062589

First Edition: February 2001

10 9 8 7 6 5 4 3 2 1

Let Your Worries Go is produced by becker&mayer!, Kirkland, Washington.
www.beckermayer.com

Illustrations by Paddy Bruce
Designed by Holly McNeill
Edited by Jennifer Doyle and Ben Raker
Production by: Cindy Curren, Barbara Galvani, and Sheila Kamuda

This book is dedicated to Grandma Arlene, who always told me that worrying was a waste of time because "you could never imagine in your wildest dreams which things will come true."

And to Miriam, The Elder, who could teach the world a thing or two about accepting the things you cannot change and having the courage to change the things you can.

becker&mayer! would also like to dedicate this book to the memory of designer Holly McNeill, whose vision illuminates these pages, and whose life touched those around her.

Acknowledgments

A million thanks to all the people who offered their guidance and support on this book so I didn't have to worry too much. I'd like to acknowledge Jennifer Doyle for her vision and ability to turn buds into blossoms. Thank you to Ben Raker, Holly McNeill, and Barbara Galvani at becker&mayer! for pushing it through the final stages; and to Paddy Bruce for providing such vibrant illustrations. Further gratitude to Elizabeth Beier at St. Martin's Press for recognizing the value of this project.

Best wishes to Lynn Gordon for all of her mentoring and encouragement. Deep appreciation for my KBHK-TV family, and also for my coworkers at ThriveOnline/Oxygen Media (for taking over while I was huddled over my laptop in the Himalayas). "*Shukriya*" and "*thugs rje che*" to the people of McCleodganj, India, for teaching me the difference between real and imagined concerns.

Many thanks to my dad for his passion for words, and to my mom for all of her "psycho-babble." A big "shmanks" to Karina for her savvy editing skills and laptop rescue in the eleventh hour. Warm fuzzies to my "Yeah-Yeahs." Gracias, Greggie, for "helping me to smile in the face of adversity." And finally, my deepest gratitude to the rest of my incredibly supportive friends and family (you know who you are)—with so much love around, I should have very little else to worry about!

Important

Worry doll powers only extend so far. For some people, worries are far more serious than they are for others. If you're having trouble managing your anxieties, you may want to consider consulting a professional therapist or doctor.

Introduction

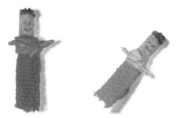

Do you bite your nails to the quick, break into a sweat when faced with a daunting deadline, or find yourself lying awake at night wondering "What if..."?

You're not alone. In this day and age, we've learned to accept high levels of stress and anxiety—much of which is caused by worrying—as the norm for productive and functional members of society. Yes, we're all busy and find ourselves feeling out of control sometimes. Sure, a little worrying is constructive when it helps you process a problem or inspires you to work that much harder. It's when compulsive worrying infringes on our daily lives—even on the fun parts—that it's time to take a step back, and let it go.

For moral support, a set of authentic Guatemalan worry dolls, sometimes called "trouble dolls," has been included with the book, along with creative ideas on how you might use them. We can all take a cue from the legend of these tiny figures. According to Guatemalan custom, if you tell each doll a different concern and place them under your pillow at night, your anxieties will have vanished by morning. Maybe it's magic, or maybe it just feels better knowing your troubles have been vocalized and shared. The number of dolls is significant—there are only six, so you limit your worries to the six most important ones each night. You should have no more, and this is all the dolls can cure.

The following pages provide the worriers of the world with light-hearted-yet-practical techniques for keeping worries in perspective. For chronic worriers, this won't be easy to do; worrying is a habit that must be broken—like quitting smoking or biting your fingernails. The moral of the story is this: some things in life cannot be planned, neatly labeled and filed away, or even explained. Why waste time fretting about things beyond your control? Rein in your practical side. Suspend the belief that whatever can go wrong, will. Let the following methods inspire you to stop being so hard on yourself and let your worries go!

Worry Journal

Molehills can turn into mountains when left to linger in a brain too long. Writing about concerns in a "worry journal" may help you gain perspective. Create a journal dedicated to fantastic fears, phony phobias, and all-consuming anxieties. This is the place for you to break down worries into little bite-size chunks you can handle. You could decorate the cover by gluing worry dolls to it, or stick them to the spine so they stand out on your shelf.

Start by making a list of all the worries that have been plaguing your thoughts. Your list might include the uneasy feeling that you won't meet a deadline, or your concern about waking up with a monster zit the morning of a big presentation. No fear is too big, too small, or too irrational to be included.

The next step is to "catastrophize" each item. What is the absolute worst outcome? Are you afraid that if you miss your deadline, you'll be fired and end up at the unemployment office? Are you worried that when the audience sees your pimple, they'll run out of the room screaming? Imagining the worst-case scenario will help you get to the root of your worries. You can also try giving each worry on your list a goofy name, such as "The Deadline that Ate New York" or "The Zit of the Century." This technique will help you to relax and take your situation a little less seriously.

Now, brainstorm the *best* possible outcome for each fear, as well as a small action you plan to take to help reach it. For example, if a larger-than-life project is causing you to panic, you might jot down that your first goal is to create an outline. Or if you're upset about a fight you had with a friend, you might document what you'd like to express to him or her. Many of your worries may have originated from the feeling that you don't have control over a situation. Taking small steps can help you feel less helpless.

The best part about a worry journal is that you can read over past entries when you're feeling anxious about a new problem. In most cases, you'll see that your worst concerns worked out just fine in the end. This should lead you to the realization that worrying is a waste of time and energy.

LET IT GO!

The traditional way to use worry dolls is to tell the dolls about your problems and keep them under your pillow at night while you sleep. But that doesn't mean you can't invent your own special "letting go" rituals using the figures. Why not tell your worries to a doll, tie the doll to the string of a helium balloon, and release the balloon and its tiny passenger into the sky? (For eco-worriers, biodegradable balloons are now available.) Or attach the doll to a piece of driftwood and toss the wood out to sea. You can also bury the dolls (and your worries) in an airtight container for a future civilization to discover.

Distraction Action

Although it isn't healthy to suppress problems, it is important to take a break from them sometimes. A mental respite can give you fresh perspective and renewed energy to tackle the issues at hand. Distractions might include an absorbing novel, an intense video game, or a cheesy movie marathon.

Films, soap operas, or books with dramatic plots can help you take your worries less seriously. After all, how bad can your problems be in comparison to a woman with a brain tumor who has a daughter with amnesia married to her husband's secret twin? Tearjerkers can be cathartic, and suspense films distract with their white-knuckler plot twists. Meanwhile, renting a comedy is perfect for the release that comes with laughter— nature's surest de-stresser.

Another good method for distraction is a hobby or chore that requires your full attention. It can be therapeutic to build a model plane, cultivate a garden, or just give the toilet a good scrubbing. Many people find that mindless repetitive actions, such as knitting or painting a fence, are meditative. You may even discover that while participating in one of these activities, your mind wanders from the task at hand and finds a solution to your problem.

11

Block it Out!

Worrywarts often get stuck in cycles of negative thought. Pesky internal voices tell you that you're not good enough, you will fail, or you should expect the worst.

The first step in breaking the unhealthy pattern is to find an activity that makes you fully conscious of the habit. Doing something unusual can help. Try finding some small wooden building blocks and keeping them at your desk or workspace. When you start to feel anxious, write the subject of your concern on one of the blocks with a marker. Then when you begin to worry about something else, jot down that trouble, and stack the new block on top of the previous one.

Continue this activity until all of the pieces (and your worries) come tumbling down. This exercise should make you more aware of the subject, frequency and duration of your pessimistic thoughts because you get to see them physically piling up. Learning to recognize the negative inner dialogue can also help you discover where it originates. Are your fears really your own, or did they come from your parents, your peers, or society as a whole?

For positive reinforcement, think up a phrase or password to stop your inner critic from ruining your fun. It could be a simple word such as "Carefree," or a more dynamic phrase such as "I am the

ep. Step with care and great tact and remember that Life's a Great Balancing Act." —Dr. Seuss

master of my universe!" Just make sure to think rather than speak your affirmation, or you might get a few weird looks.

"Are your fears really your own, or did they come from your parents, your peers, or society as a whole?"

Another method of halting negative thoughts is to distract yourself with something that requires your complete attention —like reciting the alphabet backward in your head. You'll find that by the time you reach the letter "A," you will have relaxed a bit. This is especially helpful for times when anxiety causes a physical reaction. Under duress,

you may experience an accelerated heart rate, have difficulty breathing, or break into a cold sweat. These symptoms, in turn, can make you feel even more panicky. To stop the cycle, you must stop the thoughts causing it. Silly games or distractions can help you win the battle.

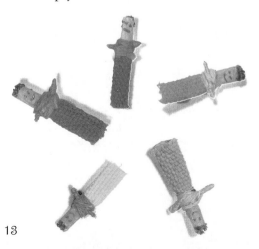

LET THE GAMES BEGIN

Playing games is a great way to lessen worry and anxiety. Try this spin on the traditional game of jacks: Get a small rubber ball, and spread the worry dolls on a smooth table. Now, using only one hand, drop the ball on the surface and try to scoop up as many of the worry dolls as you can before the ball bounces again. Try it repeatedly until you're able to pick up all of them. Smooth, repetitive activities like this can be considered active forms of meditation.

Exercise is one of the best ways to keep anxieties at bay. A fitness routine can increase your energy level—energy you need, to cope with the stresses of everyday life. The endorphins secreted when you exercise have been scientifically proven to boost your mood, which makes worrying harder to do. Exercise can also provide a break from thinking too much—a common characteristic of worriers.

Experiment with different types of exercise to find out which combats worry the best for you. Kick-boxing is a great way to vent frustration, while yoga promotes a sense of tranquillity and spiritual well-being. Walking and

npics

jogging are great activities for times when you feel like being by yourself, while team sports offer a more competitive challenge. In your worry journal, record how different types of exercise make you feel. To experience maximum benefits, you should exercise for an hour at least three times a week.

If you want to exercise your mind as well as your body, try visualization. Run as fast as you can, and imagine your worries trailing far behind, or play baseball and pretend that every pitch thrown your way is something that causes you stress. Now give the ball a satisfying whack into the outfield!

"There are many people who are always anticipating trouble, and in this way they manage to enjoy many sorrows that never really happened to them."

—*Henry Wheeler Shaw*
19th c. American humorist

Study the bigger and smaller pictures around you—from outer space to insect life—to gain perspective on the actual size of your problems. You may realize your troubles aren't all that important in the grand (or petite) scheme of things.

Take a walk in the woods and consider your surroundings. Don't forget to put some worry dolls in your pocket before you set out on your trek. Look up at the tall, ancient trees and realize that your problems will come and go, and the trees will still be standing strong. Spending time in nature is one of the best ways to make sense of the disorder in the world. The next time your worries get out of control, imagine you are a sturdy tree located in the center of a tornado. No matter how hard the wind blows, your deep roots stay grounded.

Next search out some critters to observe for at least fifteen minutes. If you're lucky, you may stumble upon a spider creating an elegant web. See how diligently she weaves the silken threads without comparing her web to her

"No matter how hard the wind blows, your deep roots stay grounded."

peers'? Follow a bee as he pollinates flowers. He seems to go about his business without worrying about the future, yet still gets the job done. What can you discover about yourself and your own life by watching these tiny creatures?

Finally, find a place where you can view the stars at night. Look up at the sky and ask yourself, "What is the actual size of my worries in comparison to the universe?" This isn't to say that your problems aren't important. Rather, it's a way to prevent you from blowing their significance out of proportion. No worry is astronomical when placed against the great, starry sky.

Worry Stones

Rub away worries with a worry stone, a long-standing

American Indian tradition. Hematite is most often known

as the "worry stone," because it is believed to have

healing properties that alleviate worry and anxiety.

Agate and smoky quartz are thought to be good for grounding and balance. Amethyst is used to calm an overactive mind, the curse of many worrywarts. Aquamarine, turquoise, and emerald are used to induce tranquillity, banish fears, and calm nervous tension. If personal stress or inner confusion bog you down, consider finding some azurite.

All of these stones make good worry stones, but any small, flat, smooth one will do. If you want your special stone to have a glossy finish, shine it with rock polish. Whenever you feel anxious, cradle the stone in your fingers and stroke it with your thumb. Close your eyes and become aware of the weight, texture, and temperature of the rock. Imagine that it is absorbing all your negativity and anxiety. If you rub the same spot every time, eventually the friction from your fingers rubbing against it will wear a comfortable groove in the rock.

You can use your worry stone when you're stuck in traffic, during a stressful meeting, or in any situation where you feel tense. Worry stones are particularly helpful for fidgeters who need an outlet for their nervous energy. Think of the stone as your own secret security blanket.

Talk It Out

" Don't find a fault. Find

Whether you confide in a friend,

a worry doll, a therapist, or your

pet iguana, communicating trou-

bles to others is important for

sound mental health and clarity

of thought.

Without outside perspective, it's easy to obsess—your brain filled with the same nagging thoughts going round and round without resolution. An objective listener may be able to give you the insight needed to break closed-circuit thought patterns, help brainstorm solutions, and realize when you are blowing problems out of proportion. It also feels good to know that you aren't alone in solving the issues that are bothering you. You may even discover that others have experienced similar situations and can offer helpful advice. Be sure to reciprocate, as listening to a friend's problems can be a great way to temporarily forget your own. Try swapping anxieties with someone you trust—tackle her tough problems while she takes on yours!

If you feel your anxiety level is out of control, consult a therapist. A professional can help you to identify the symptoms of a real anxiety disorder and to break unhealthy thought patterns you can't seem to kick on your own.

As for talking to your pet, just verbalizing your fears—especially to a creature that's not judgmental—can help you get a grasp on them. Pets have been known to alleviate stress, and even lower blood pressure. Also, the fact that you're talking to an animal may help you take the situation just a little bit less seriously. After all, how many fuzzy critters get worked up about debt, relationship troubles, or deadlines?

21

ROAD RAGE REMEDY

How often do you find yourself stuck in traffic, worrying that you'll be late for an appointment? Or flying off the handle when another driver cuts you off? If these situations sound all too familiar, a few friendly faces can remind you to stay calm behind the wheel. Tie some worry dolls to your key chain with a loop of thread, or let them dangle from your rearview mirror. The next time you feel a case of road rage creeping up, resist the urge to curse and wave your arms like a maniac. Instead, hold the dolls in your hand, take deep breaths, and wait for your sanity to return.

The Worry Zone

Pick a designated time and place to fret

about your troubles. The purpose of the

"worry zone" is to get all the worrying

out of your system in one shot so it

doesn't invade other aspects of your life.

It also gives you an outlet so you don't

worry all the time.

First choose a comfortable spot where you can worry without interruption. Your worry zone might be a favorite chair, a fireplace hearth, or a tree fort you build yourself. You might want to make your own "Do Not Disturb—Worry Session in Progress" sign to hang there.

Set aside a specific amount of "worry time" each day. It could be fifteen minutes, or up to an hour if you have a lot on your mind. Now all you need to do is worry: dwell on the fact that you can't afford your mortgage, obsess about the obvious signs that you have some rare disease, torment yourself with the knowledge that your mother is coming to stay with you for two whole weeks. You don't need a planned agenda—just let your mind wander through the different issues that have been dampening your joie de vivre. Pay special attention to how you feel when each topic crosses your mind. You may discover that a small concern has been bothering you more than you realized. Keep your worry journal handy so you can jot down revelations as they come to you.

"...dwell on the fact that you can't afford your mortgage, obsess about the obvious signs that you have some rare disease, torment yourself with the knowledge that your mother is coming to stay..."

Set an alarm clock so you'll know when worry time is up. When the buzzer goes off, you aren't permitted to worry anymore! If you have unresolved thoughts, put them on paper, and on the following day, pick up where you left off. After your session, plan a fun activity to reward yourself for taking the time to address your tensions instead of letting them build up.

Creative Expression

"Worry a little bit every day and in a lifetime you will lose a couple of years. If something is wrong, fix it if you can. But train yourself not to worry. Worry never fixes anything."

—Mary Hemingway

You may not be the next Picasso, but expressing your fears and troubles through creativity can be therapeutic. Draw, paint, sculpt, or write a story about the things that are bothering you. Giving your concerns tangible form can make them appear more manageable. It is also a cathartic way to purge them from your system.

While molding a piece of clay, think about the fight you had with your mother, or your bad evaluation at work, and see what shape evolves. You might also keep crayons and paper in areas where you tend to stress, such as near the phone. That way, the next

time you have a worrisome conversation, you can doodle to take the edge off.

"Giving your concerns a tangible form can make them appear more manageable."

If you find creativity especially beneficial, consider taking art therapy classes. You may be surprised at what you discover about yourself and learn from the other participants in the group.

If art isn't your thing, write a story about your worries, complete with a cheerful, fairy-tale ending. Inventing your own fiction can help you feel as if you have control over a situation, and can also be an outlet for actions you are unable to take in real life. Do you fantasize about leaving the rat race and living on a tropical island? In reality, many obligations may keep you from buying a one-way ticket to Hawaii, but in a story you can do anything you want, no matter how impractical. Don a lei and give it a try!

TINY ALTARS

Many cultures and religions create altars expressly for meditation. Build your own unique "antiworry" shrine in your home or office. Decorate a shoe box or a shelf with worry dolls and other items that help reduce your stress level. Whenever an anxiety attack strikes, sit in front of your altar until you achieve a more serene state of mind. Light candles and incense to complete your stress-busting ritual. To create a portable "mini-shrine," just put a few worry dolls in a matchbox with other stress-reducing charms, such as tiny worry stones or inspirational quotations clipped from a magazine.

An antiworry kit is a first-aid kit for worriers.

The act of gathering its contents can itself

help you relax and prepare you for handling

anxieties. Here you can practice creative

expression and prepare to face your fears.

To create your own kit, get a shoe box or basket, and fill it with things that combat your worries. It might include soothing, significant, or powerful items such as your worry dolls, a postcard from your wise grandmother, relaxing bubble bath, that tape of

Cuban music you love, a list of affirmations or inspirational quotations, or a lemon-scented candle that reminds you of a clean house. It might also contain comforting things such as chamomile tea, chocolate chip cookies, a special stuffed animal, a shell from your most relaxing tropical vacation, cozy wool socks, or a picture of your most supportive friends (your "fan club"). The objects you put in the kit should be completely personal because everybody has their own favorite comforts.

The items you select don't always have to be sentimental; they can also be symbolic. You could add a key to symbolize unlocking your hidden strengths, a mirror for seeing your inner beauty, a rock to ground you to the earth, a feather to represent feeling light and carefree, etc. With this box full of remedies, you should be well equipped for even the most severe worry emergency.

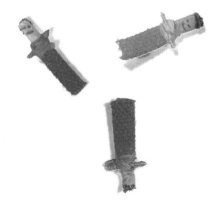

The Worry Box

Create a "worry box" where you can store worries until you're ready to process them. The box can be anything from a leftover Chinese-food container to a fancy jewelry box. Glue a few of the worry dolls to the top or sides of your special vessel. Write your concerns on separate pieces of paper and keep them in the box. When life seems overwhelming, draw a "worry card" from the container and, for ten minutes, worry about the subject written on the card. This allows you to focus on one thing at a time, preventing you from becoming overwhelmed by the multitude of concerns cluttering your brain. Plus, it's exciting to toss out cards that don't worry you anymore!

Keeping a worry box can also help you identify patterns to your worrying. Categorize your qualms and keep track of what kind are most frequently added to the box.

Do you tend to worry about things that are beyond your control?

Do you fret about the unknown? Is fear of failure a recurring theme? Perhaps your concerns are about money, or relationships? Record any personal revelations that come out of these reflective thought sessions in your worry journal. You may be surprised at the patterns that develop.

Go With the Flow

"We are, perhaps, uniquely among the earth's creatures, the worrying animal. We worry away our lives, fearing the future, discontent with the present, unable to take in the idea of dying, unable to sit still."

—*Lewis Thomas,*
American author-physician

Worrying often springs from trying to control everything all the time. Even though it's important to take charge of your life, it's equally valuable to know when to let go. Trying to be perfect all the time is a Sisyphian endeavor (you know, he's the guy who was doomed to eternally push the boulder up the mountain).

So go ahead and let things slide! Let the house get messy, pay the bills a little late, don't balance your checkbook for a while. You will realize that your life won't go to pieces if you aren't in control all the time. And if things do fall apart, you'll learn that you're capable of putting them back together again.

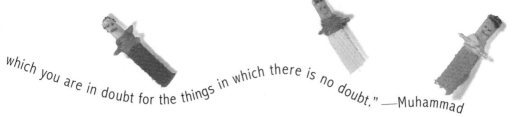

"Letting go" doesn't come easily to most worrywarts. Start by choosing a specific day and consciously deciding to go with the flow on that day alone. Don't make plans ahead of time—make decisions as they are presented to you. You may be pleasantly surprised to discover where the day takes you.

Because worriers frequently fear they won't be able to deal with unexpected events, they often ruminate on every possible outcome until they drive themselves batty. This is impossible to do if you choose to take things as they come, or to "cross that bridge when you come to it."

When you stop trying to control every moment of your day, you will be amazed at how much time and energy you have left to enjoy life. It's like swimming in a stream; it's exhausting to battle the current, but floating along with it is a delight!

Natural Remedies

Many people find that herbs, vitamins, and scents are effective means for controlling anxiety. The next time you're feeling uptight, try unwinding with a cup of chamomile tea (known for its relaxing effect). Kava kava, valerian root, St. John's wort, ginseng, and catnip are other herbs thought to have calming properties (make sure to consult with your doctor before using). Vitamin B and niacin are recommended by many in the medical field to help combat stress and promote a healthy nervous system.

In aromatherapy, different scents are used to promote relaxation. Essential oils can be used for an antiworry bath, diffused into the air with an oil burner, or even dabbed on your wrist so you can take a whiff whenever you need to tame tension. Stock up on lavender-scented essential oils, candles, and incense—some people find the smell encourages relaxation and a sense of well-being.

Other scents known for their sedative qualities include benzoin, bergamot, chamomile, cedar wood, clary sage, cypress, frankincense, geranium, hyssop, jasmine, juniper, marjoram, melissa, neroli, patchouli, rosewood, sandalwood, verbena, vetivert, and ylang ylang. When anxiety leads to exhaustion, rosemary, black pepper, peppermint, and thyme are frequently recommended to restore energy. Experiment with different aromas to discover which ones diminish your worry monster. To make an especially powerful worry-extinguisher, place potpourri in a bowl along with a couple of drops of essential oil, and set your worry dolls around the edges.

ACCESSORIZE YOUR WORRIES AWAY

Set a new fashion trend by making your own worry-doll accessories. For a pair of unique earrings, simply hang the Guatemalan figures from earring hooks (available at craft stores). To create an eclectic worry-necklace, attach several of your helpful pals to a piece of colorful thread, then tie it around your neck. Or make an ankle bracelet that you can wear without observation, for those days when you want to keep your worries to yourself. You can also use the dolls to make fanciful pins. With your new worry jewelry close at hand, you'll have nearby support if you start feeling anxious or overwhelmed.

Healthy Living

"Worry affects the circulation, the heart, the glands, the whole nervous system. I have never known a man who died from overwork, but many who died from doubt."

—Dr. Charles Horace Mayo,
cofounder of the Mayo Clinic

Dr. Mayo's theory works both ways—worrying excessively can make you physically ill, and a run-down physique can itself be quite worrisome. When we are sick, it is easy for troubles to seem insurmountable because we don't have enough energy to deal with them. Staying fit and healthy through diet and exercise can help you tackle life's little annoyances.

Never underestimate the importance of a well-balanced diet, which means eating a wide variety of foods in moderation. You may have special "comfort foods" that you turn to when you want to feel warm and safe. For some, it's cookies and milk, and for others

it's tomato soup like mom used to make. Indulging in treats is fine once in a while, but be careful that you don't start using food as a means to avoid dealing with problems. Also, go easy on the junk food, as many people experience a "low" after a sugar "high." Try satisfying your sweet tooth with dried or fresh fruit instead of candy.

Keep substances such as caffeine, alcohol, and nicotine to a minimum. Excess caffeine can intensify the symptoms of high anxiety, including a rapid pulse and shakiness. It can also disrupt your sleep patterns and contribute to insomnia. Alcohol is a depressant that can contribute to feelings of hopelessness.

Many people are under the impression that a nightcap or cigarette will help them sleep when they're feeling wound-up, but the truth is that drinking alcohol interferes with a deep, sound slumber. Cigarette addiction can cause mood swings and physical and mental withdrawals, which are not conditions that should be cultivated by worry-warts. Have you ever seen anyone as nervous and jittery as a smoker trying to quit?

Worry Beads

Greeks often run their fingers over komboloi, *or worry beads, to alleviate stress. The tradition of carrying strings of beads is said to have originated in India as a way of counting prayers, but it is practiced in many different cultures and religions all over the world.*

To make your own set of worry beads, place about twenty pea-size beads on a leather or nylon string, and tie the ends together like a necklace. Whenever you start to worry, grasp one of the beads next to the knot, and hold it between your thumb and index finger. Then, move your fingers down the strand to the next bead, and silently continue counting each one. If you still feel anxious by the time you reach the last bead, start the process all over again. After some practice, the repetitive motion will become second nature. This ritual keeps fidgety fingers busy, while the act of counting crowds worrisome voices out of your head.

Many people close their eyes while using worry beads, while others mindlessly run their fingers over the strands while stuck in traffic or while having conversations. One of the many benefits of this antiworry method is that you can easily carry your beads with you, so they are readily available wherever you need them—at home, at the office, or in the car.

ON THE JOB

If you tend to have a lot of stress in your workplace, think of different ways you can incorporate the worry dolls into your job. If you are a doctor, attach them to your lab coat or stethoscope to ease your own anxieties and bring a smile to patients' faces. If you are a dentist, glue the tiny figures onto the ends of toothbrushes, and give them to fearful clients. Teachers and students alike can attach the little antiworry helpers to their notebooks or file folders. How might you be able to use the worry dolls in your career? No matter where you work, the dolls are always on the job when it comes to reducing anxiety!

"Laughter is an instant vacation."

—Milton Berle, American comedian

As we grow older and our responsibilities increase, many of us forget how to laugh and play. It's easier to take your problems less seriously if you don't take *yourself* too seriously. Whenever you feel a worry attack creeping up, try throwing on a pair of Groucho Marx glasses or a silly outfit, and telling your troubles to your image in a mirror. You won't be able to keep a straight face for long. If this doesn't do the trick, try renting a few goofy videos, going out to a comedy club, or reading the funnies in the Sunday paper.

Best Medicine

hee-hee! hee-hee! hee-hee!

It's important to take time out of your hectic schedule to play. Why not gather together a group of friends on a weekly or monthly basis for "game night"? Whether it's poker, charades, or cribbage, you'll find that these games are terrific ways to reduce stress.

"It's easier to take your problems less seriously if you don't take *yourself* too seriously."

Rediscovering your inner kid will also assist in the battle against worry. Ever notice how easy it is to make a child smile? Maybe it's time you regressed a little. Think about things that used to give you great pleasure before life got too complicated. Was it having ice cream on a hot day or running barefoot in the grass? Did you enjoy letting your fingers squish through finger paints or clay? Your imagination is the limit! After a good stretch (so you don't hurt your aging body), try rolling down a hill or springing a cartwheel. You'll be grinning from ear to ear in no time.

Acts of Kindness

> *"The best cure for worry, depression, melancholy, brooding, is to go deliberately forth and try to lift with one's sympathy the gloom of somebody else."*
> —*Arnold Bennett,*
> *19th c. British novelist*

People may tell you that your problems aren't terribly serious in comparison to the hardships of others in the world, but it's tough to understand what this means until you've experienced it firsthand. Volunteering to help those less fortunate than yourself is also a great way to remind yourself of the things in life you take for granted. To be truly thankful for your food and home, lend a hand at a homeless shelter. To be grateful for your health, spend some time at an AIDS hospice. To appreciate your youth, volunteer at a nursing home.

If you really want to value your freedom, get involved in political activism, defending people who have had their basic human rights taken away.

When you volunteer, take time to listen to the people you're helping. Ask them what they worry about, and it may make your troubles feel insignificant in comparison. Many impoverished people work so hard to have their basic needs met that finding time to worry is actually a luxury. You might also discover that others who have survived horrific experiences only fret when *really* big problems arise.

If you don't have the time to volunteer, practicing random and not-so-random acts of kindness is another great way to help others while making yourself feel good at the same time. It feels especially good to do nice things for others and not tell anyone that you did them—like a secret elf. That way, you aren't doing the good deeds for recognition, but just to help out someone in need (and maybe to boost your spirits a bit). Try leaving flowers for somebody who is having a rough time, feeding a parking meter that is about to expire, or anonymously donating money to a cause that you feel is important.

DOLLS OF PROTEST, DOLLS FOR JUSTICE

On March 21, 1996, student groups across the United States held teach-ins and demonstrations to show solidarity with Guatemalan student activists protesting human-rights abuses in their homeland. As part of the effort, which was coordinated by the nonprofit group Amnesty International, students in both countries made hundreds of worry dolls to protest the beatings, rapes, deaths, and disappearances of more than 140,000 Guatemalans during thirty-six years of civil war. Amnesty International continues the quest for justice and truth, and seeks the further declassification of U.S. government documents revealing the CIA's role in Central America's unrest. To find out how you can help fight human-rights abuses in Guatemala and around the world, call Amnesty International at 1-800-AMNESTY, or write to Amnesty International USA, ATTN: Member Services Department, 322 Eighth Avenue, Tenth Floor, New York, NY 10001; http://www.amnesty-usa.org.

Rate Your Worries

Worrying can be productive when it helps us come up with a solution to a problem. Excessive worrying, on the other hand, can be harmful and actually decrease our ability to handle a situation effectively. It can cause us to lose perspective on the importance of our problems, allowing tiny issues to become huge ones in our minds.

To counteract this phenomenon, spend some time mulling over the actual size of each problem you have, and decide which ones are really that dire.

Make a list of all your worries. Next, rate the importance of each issue, using a scale of 1 through 10. Assign the number 1 to the most minor problems, and give a 10 to the most serious. Give a parking ticket a low score, for example, and a serious illness a much higher ranking. Scoring should be subjective, based on your feelings alone—don't rate them based on what others might think. When you're finished, take a good, hard look at the issues you deemed most serious.

Next make a list of your priorities in life, in order of importance. Priorities should include both the things you need and the things you want—food, shelter, health, family, friends, career, freedom, money, creativity, physical fitness, etc. When you are finished, compare the two lists. Do the concerns at the top of your worry list match up with the ones on your priority list? If not, you might want to reassess the amount of energy you have been devoting to each of your troubles. Think about limiting your worries to six per day (the maximum daily allowance, according to worry-doll legend). This might help you limit your concern on problems that are really important. Remember that "good" worrying is nothing more than a form of focused thought. Concentrate on constructive worrying by making your lists and getting rid of things you don't need to waste time thinking about. Try the exercise again in a few months to discover if any of your priorities have changed.

Simple Pleasures

When worries feel too complex or overwhelming, counteract them by becoming aware of the simple pleasures in life. To do this, start a list in your worry journal of all the small things that make life worthwhile. You can create a master list or simply write down three things you're thankful for at the end of each day. It might be the elderly woman who smiled at you on your way to work; snowflakes melting on your tongue; bubble baths; your favorite team scoring a touchdown; or watermelon on a summer day. You'll be surprised at how many wonderful things life has to offer when you choose to focus on the positives instead of the negatives.

Carry your worry journal with you so you can write down the little joys as you encounter them, and so you'll have it on hand when you need a reminder of how beautiful life can be. You might also want to share your list with friends, who can remind you of some special things you've overlooked.

44

"There are two days in the week about which and upon which I never worry.... One of these days is Yesterday.... And the other day I do not worry about is Tomorrow."

—Robert Jones Burdette,
19th c. American writer

SURPRISE YOURSELF

If you're having an especially stressful week, make yourself a Guatemalan greeting card. Fold a sheet of colorful construction paper in half, and write your favorite inspirational poem or saying inside. Affix several of the worry dolls to the front of the card, and mail it to your home or work address. Even though you'll know the card is on the way, receiving a ray of sunshine in the mail will brighten your day.

Through the Ages

Spending time with children or elders is a good reality check when it comes to worrying. Most youngsters have little capacity to worry, because they only know how to live in the present moment. They also have a knack for appreciating the little pleasures in life, which are easy to forget as we grow older. If you don't have children of your own, offer to baby-sit for a friend or family member. Many hospitals also have volunteer positions for "baby rockers." It's virtually impossible to fret while sitting in a rocking chair lulling an infant to sleep.

Elders, on the other hand, can teach you that life is too short to be consumed by anxieties. On your deathbed, do you want to look back at your time on this planet and realize you spent it worrying instead of living life to the fullest? Probably not.

Spending time with the elderly— whether they are older relatives, or residents of a nursing home you visit—can be beneficial for everyone involved. Take the time to listen to the advice elders have to offer; they can allow you insight into many of the problems you face because they have lived through similar ones. It is possible to learn from the mistakes of others instead of wasting time making them yourself.

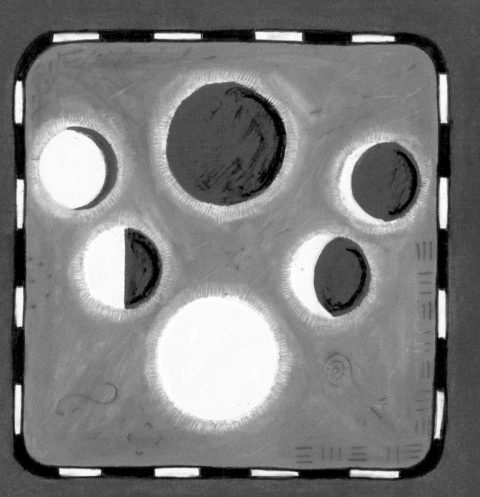

Travel more, Worry less

"Worry is like a rocking chair: it gives you something to do, but it doesn't get you anywhere."

—Unknown

Taking a trip is a terrific way to temporarily escape your troubles. You don't need to go somewhere exotic to go on vacation—in fact, you don't even need to leave your hometown. Just do something to break out of your daily routine. Visit someplace nearby where you rarely venture. Do something you usually wouldn't dare. Take a trip to the museum, or go to the zoo. If you are a closet rock star, try a karaoke bar.

The most important part about going on vacation—either mental or physical—is that you leave your work and worries behind. On vacation, it's easy to live in the present and pretend that bills, bosses, and life's other little annoyances don't exist. Don't forget to pack your worry dolls when you go.

Lying on a tropical beach with a fruity drink in hand is not the only way to diminish stress. Although taking a trip to a big city may not seem like a good way to get rid of worries, it can be. It might even give you more worries to begin with, such as missing flights, losing luggage, or getting robbed. Still, these fears will be different than your ordinary ones, and they

may be strangely simpler. Conquering new problems on unfamiliar ground can make you feel empowered when you return home to everyday life. If you can handle these challenges while out of your "comfort zone," other obstacles may seem more manageable by comparison.

Traveling to a foreign country presents challenges, as well—especially if you travel in the Third World. But it can also help you realize that you don't have it so bad after all. Use the experience to reassess your priorities. You may not have a lot of money, the perfect job, or the best figure—but if you have your freedom, food, shelter, and love, you have very little else to worry about!

WRITE ON!

Think of all the stressful things you do with a pen in your hand: writing reports, paying the bills, filling out tax forms, etc. Even writing meant to purge concerns can backfire when you're too careful with your prose. It doesn't have to be this way. Next time, be ready for those wordsmith's worries with a doll-enhanced writing implement. Just glue a worry doll or two to the cap of your pen or to the side of your pencil. These decorative tools also make terrific gifts for the other worrywarts in your life. They can help keep things in perspective when you're fretting over finances or putting the final touches on the world's next best-seller.

Daily Affirmations

"What, me worry?"
—Alfred E. Neuman,
"Mad" magazine

Daily affirmations are a great way to help you stay positive when challenging situations strike. Make a deck of cards you can draw upon to remind you of your strengths and to give you strategies to deal with worries spiraling out of control.

Cut pieces of colorful poster board into one-by-three-inch strips. Then write down one word on each card, such as "spontaneity," "trust," "courage," or "release." You can also include little reminders of ways to face worries, like "Cross that bridge when I get to it," "Think positively," or "Go with the flow." Even if these concepts seem obvious, we often forget that they are real options. The cards can help us remember. For extra effect, glue a worry doll to the cards to enhance their healing powers.

Now cut out images from magazines that give you a sense of relaxation and well-being, and glue them to the outside of a small box. Put the affirmations into this container, and when worries surface, pull out a card at random. Carry it in your pocket, and meditate on the positive word(s) throughout your day.

If you don't have your antiworry cards handy, you can also write empowering phrases on small pieces of paper, and post them in conspicuous places around your home or office. Or choose a positive affirmation for a scrolling screensaver message on your computer at work—the perfect place to post a phrase to help you cope with on-the-job concerns.

Another variation of the antiworry cards is to create a little "coping toolbox"—instead of writing down affirmations on the cards, insert your favorite worry-busting methods, like writing in a journal, calling a friend, or exercising. You can draw from the techniques in this book or come up with some of your own. Then, whenever you feel your anxiety level rising, just reach into the container to discover which soothing activity you should try.

WORRY WAND

Do you fantasize about whisking worries away with a magic wand? Create your own worry wand by gluing worry dolls onto a smooth stick and decorating it with ribbons, glitter, and colorful paints. You can even invent your own magic spell to chant while waving the wand. Or pass on the unique staff to a friend who is plagued by anxieties. Your friend can pass the gift back to you when he or she is feeling better, or keep the support network going by handing it off to another worrier.

Dream Worries Away

Have you noticed how even small things bother you when you don't get enough sleep? Take the time to really listen to your body, consider how much shut-eye it requires, and plan accordingly.

To ensure a good night's sleep and regulate your body clock, try to go to bed at around the same time every night. Also, be aware that the temperature, light, and sound filtering into your room can affect sleep quality. You may need to invest in a good pair of earplugs to drown out your noisy neighbor's booming stereo, or get a tape or CD featuring nature sounds or white noise to soothe yourself into slumber land. A small fan or sound machine can create calming white noise, as can a miniature bedside fountain. Remember to try voicing your concerns to the dolls and putting them under you pillow to help your sleep. If you have a tough time falling asleep because you can't stop ruminating on the worries of your day, get out of bed and do something relaxing, such as reading a book or listening to mellow music. Get back into bed when you start to feel drowsy.

Once you do manage to sleep, pay attention to the dreams that you have; they might help give you insight into the root of your worries. There are many books available that can help you recognize the symbolism in your dreams. As a start, here are the meanings behind a few common anxiety dreams. Do you recognize any of these symbols?

❧ *Dreams where you are submerged in water or caught in the middle of a storm may represent feeling overwhelmed by life and daily experiences.*

❧ *If mountains, walls, and fences frequently appear in your dreams, you might have obstacles or challenges to overcome.*

❧ *Have you ever had a dream where you just can't move, no matter how hard you try? This paralysis might represent fears of things outside your control.*

❧ *Paths, roads, and stairs are thought to be representative of your direction in life—traveling in an upward direction is*

supposed to be a good, but going downward may mean you need to reevaluate a choice you've made.

❧ *If you're experiencing feelings of confusion, you may find yourself dreaming of mazes.*

❧ *Mirrors in dreams can represent self-examination.*

❧ *Bosses in dreams can symbolize your inner critic.*

❧ *If you dream that you're running away from somebody, you may not be ready to face a situation.*

Keep your worry journal by your bed, and record your nightly visions as soon as you wake up.

DEADLINE DOLLS

Do you frequently worry about forgetting deadlines or important appointments? Let your worry dolls serve as cheerful reminders. You could glue one to some yarn to tie around your finger (or wrist) so the big meeting won't slip your mind. You could also write down on notecards the things that you want to remember and attach a paper clip with a doll glued to the ends. The brightly colored figure should catch your attention so you won't forget to read the message. Put the cards next to your alarm clock so they are the first thing you see when you wake up. This will decrease your nighttime anxiety, making it easier to drift off into a peaceful sleep.

"Be master of your petty annoyances

and conserve your energies for the big,

worthwhile things. It isn't the mountain

ahead that wears you out—it's the grain

of sand in your shoe."

—Robert Service, Canadian poet

Many of us worry when we're disorganized, because disorganization can lead to losing things, missing deadlines, or being late for important appointments. If these situations sound familiar, you may need to take stock of your organizational impairments and compensate accordingly.

If you frequently lose your keys, you might try getting a few spare sets made so you don't have to fret when you're running late in the morning. If you tend to forget important dates, keep a large calendar with colorful markers in a conspicuous place. Stick worry dolls to your calendar to mark important days. Subscribe to a Web site that will e-mail you reminders so you don't forget paperwork. You might also set up a simple filing system so you'll be able to locate important documents when you need them.

If you chronically run late, learning to manage time effectively will help reduce your stress and worry. Don't overschedule, and leave early for appointments, allowing a cushion for unexpected delays. Prioritizing a to-do list can also help you make better use of your time, so you aren't always left scrambling to pull things together at the last minute. Figure out what time of day you're the most productive and alert. Plan to tackle your most difficult projects during these high-efficiency hours.

Simplify Your Life

One of the best things you can do to reduce fretting is to "simplify your life" or "get back to basics." Spend some time figuring out the differences between your wants and your needs. Maybe you'll discover that you can take a lower-paying job and ditch the power career that saps you of all your precious energy. Or maybe you'll come up with smaller ways to simplify, such as buying clothes that don't need to be dry-cleaned or getting rid of appliances that require a lot of maintenance.

Using technology wisely can help make life more manageable, but it can also be a double-edged sword. It can reduce your stress level by making work more efficient, but sometimes the amount of information you receive, the maintenance involved, or the price tag attached can be overwhelming.

Try cutting out technology for a week to find out what equipment or services you really need. You might even try avoiding electricity for a night, and go about your activities by candlelight to see how it feels. Revel in the serene silence that replaces the booming stereo, jabbering television, and ringing phone. This experiment can also provide you with an opportunity to spend quality time with your family, playing games or just talking. Reconnecting with loved ones can help to limit stress.

> "Who is General Failure and why is he reading my hard drive?"
>
> —Unknown

The TV might provide you with hours of great distraction, but it can also take time away from activities that are rejuvenating to the self, such as exercising or hanging out with friends. Likewise, e-mail may be an efficient way to get messages to friends, family, and business associates, but it also means missing out on the personal connection that comes with visits, phone calls, and even letters. It may seemed old-fashioned, but taking time out to write a letter is relaxing—and if the recipient replies, you will experience the excitement of receiving something in the mail other than bills. Experiment to find out how technology best serves—or doesn't serve—your personal needs.

DESKTOP HELPERS

If you work at a computer all day, it might be helpful to decorate your workstation with worry dolls. The next time your computer crashes and you lose the "most important document in the world," try giving one of the dolls a little rub to stop your blood pressure from soaring sky-high. Or when you're stuck on a project, use the dolls as a reminder to stay calm and relaxed until you find a detour around your mental block.

Worry-Free Environment

Many of us don't realize how intensely the environment around us affects our stress and worry levels. Look around your home and work space, and take note of your surroundings. The noise level, lighting, and functionality of your space might be contributing to your agitation.

If your living area is too noisy, it can lead to difficulty concentrating, relaxing, or sleeping. If you live on a loud street, there are many different methods available for soundproofing rooms. When roommates or children are the problem, you might want to call a meeting at which you establish a few daily "quiet hours." Earplugs,

headphones, or a small bedside fountain are other good tools for drowning out unwanted sounds.

The quality of light can affect your mood as well. If you're not getting enough exposure to sunlight, you might find yourself lethargic and unable to cope with stress. Artificial lighting, especially fluorescent, has also been known to make people feel agitated. The color of a room can affect your feelings. Bright colors can make you feel cheerful, whereas dark ones can bring you down. In color psychology, studies have shown that most people find blues to be most relaxing. Greens and oranges are thought to ease stress and anxiety, while purples soothe fear. Yellow is often associated with feelings of harmony. Because color preference is personal, play with different shades to find out which ones give you a positive frame of mind.

Those who practice *feng shui* believe in using the ancient art of object placement to live harmoniously with the energy in one's surroundings. This means that the way a living space is designed can change the way the energy flows in a room. People who are guided by feng shui feel that arranging your environment can have a profound effect on your moods and even life events. "Masters" in this decorative style often use plants, mirrors, and fountains to balance the fluidity of the energy in a space. It's also beneficial to keep clutter to a minimum and make sure doors and windows aren't obstructed.

A room with good feng shui should be aesthetically pleasing to you and to guests, as well as functional and environmentally sound. As the practice is based on the elements (earth, water, air, and fire), finding decorative inspiration in nature is encouraged. There are many books on feng shui. For starters, you might try *Clear Your Clutter with Feng Shui,* by Karen Kingston (Broadway Books, 1999), or one of many titles by Feng Shui expert Lillian Too.

Change the Things you Can

60

"You gain strength, courage, and con-

fidence by every experience in which you

really stop to look fear in the face. You

are able to say to yourself, 'I lived

through this horror. I can take the next

thing that comes along.' …You must do

the thing you think you cannot do."

—*Eleanor Roosevelt*

Fear and worry go hand-in-hand. To reduce anxiety, face your fears head-on!

Because worries often stem from things we feel we can't control, find out if there are things you can do to empower yourself. This could take the form of research or action. Are you troubled about your finances? Take an accounting class, or meet with a financial adviser. Are you afraid of giving a speech? Practice in front of family or talk into a tape recorder.

Many worrywarts subconsciously think that fretting is the same as preparation—"If I think about the situation enough, I'll be prepared for the outcome." But since we can't predict the end results with accuracy, we're wasting precious energy. Taking real steps, no matter how small, will help you feel more secure.

Another approach is to put yourself in a situation where you have no choice but to tackle the thing that worries you. If large crowds make you anxious, make a point of going to a packed mall or concert. If you're uncomfortable being alone, take yourself to dinner or to the movies once a week. Feel free to bring your worry dolls if you need a little moral support. Start with small steps, and eventually attempt to confront your deepest fears. You'll find that every time you confront the issue it gets easier, because you progressively grow more desensitized when nothing dire happens to you.

FRAME YOUR WORRIES

Who do you worry about? Your child? Your mom? Your spouse? A friend? Your dog? To help ease your fears, place a picture of the person (or critter) that you fret over in a plain frame. Then, decorate the border by gluing worry dolls around it. Experiment with colorful paints and glitter to create a fancier frame. You could also use the figures to decorate the cover of a photo album. Inside, you might want to include snapshots of carefree times when worries didn't seem so overwhelming.

WORRY WARDENS

Want to ward off worries at your doorstep? Hang a wreath festooned with worry dolls on your front door, or even around your doorbell. You can either glue the dolls to a pre-existing wicker wreath, or form the basic ring from plastic foam, cardboard, or wood. Cut out the center of any circular item you have around the house. A clean cardboard pizza wheel might work. Fancy cheeses come in large wooden wheels—check at your grocery store to see if they are throwing any away. For small totems to encircle doorbells, you can use a yogurt container lid. Decorate the ring with fabric, yarn, or garlands, and finally, glue the dolls around the edge. If you are a skilled wood-weaver, you could make a wicker wreath yourself. Place the dolls side-to-side holding hands, or spread them out around the circle. Then tack your wreath to the door and dare worries to enter!

Worry Dump

The sheer number of worries swirling around in our heads often becomes overwhelming. This is because we continue to add new worries without discarding old ones. Every day, make a list of six things that are troubling you (one for each worry doll), and only allow yourself to fret about the concerns on the list. Put the rest of your problems, issues, and concerns on the back burner to deal with at another time. The following day, swap one or all of the worries on your list for new ones. Today, you may worry about paying your bills, a fight you had with your significant other, or your annual evaluation at work. Tomorrow, you may have made up with your sweetie and can replace that concern with a completely new one.

It's best to write down your worries as soon as you wake up so you stay focused on real concerns, and so you don't forget which troubles you're allowed to fret over. This step can be important when you want to dump worries later. When a worry is outdated, you can take pleasure in crossing it off your list.

Another method for dumping worries is to write down the stream-of-consciousness dialogue that runs through your head when you're anxious about something. This means that you write out your thoughts as you think them, with no editing at all—you just let ideas flow like a stream. It might look something like this:

My throat is starting to hurt. What if I get sick again and can't go to work? My boss will be angry since I've just been out on vacation, and my department is short-handed. My stressed-out coworkers will have to finish my big project, and will probably resent me....

Maybe after reading your thought process on paper, you will gain a better understanding of how it works—or at least you'll realize that you're more neurotic than Woody Allen. After trying the stream-of-consciousness exercise on paper, attempt to do the same thing verbally, speaking your unedited thoughts and worries into a tape recorder. Taping yourself is great for downplaying problems because when you play the tape back, you're likely to realize how trivial it all sounds.

Progressive Relaxation

When you're anxious, it's not just your mind that tenses up—your muscles also absorb your tension. Because it's impossible to be both tense and relaxed at the same time, learning relaxation methods can help combat your worrying ways.

One way to relax is to close your eyes and imagine your body as a big bag of sand or an hourglass. Pretend there is a tiny hole in the bag at the bottom of your toe, and that you can feel grains slowly trickling out. Let this process take as long as you need it to, and become aware of all parts of your body as the sand flows on by them. By the time all of the sand is gone, much of your stress will have diminished, and your body should be completely relaxed.

Another technique, called *progressive relaxation*, is often used by psychotherapists to promote deep muscular relaxation. Progressive relaxation can also be particularly beneficial to people battling insomnia. The exercise involves contracting, and then releasing different muscle groups throughout the body.

First find a quiet place where you can lie down. Close your eyes, and start by becoming conscious of your right hand. While inhaling, squeeze your hand into a fist, and hold it for five seconds. Take note of the sensations in your hand before exhaling and releasing the fist. Now, concentrate on how different your muscles feel when they are relaxed. Next, take a deep breath, and make your entire right arm tense for five seconds. Exhale, while gradually allowing your arm to relax for the count of five. Follow the same process with your left hand and arm, paying close attention to the feeling of relaxation you experience after contracting and releasing the muscles.

Continue tensing and relaxing the rest of the muscle groups in your body, including your legs, gluts, abs, shoulders, and neck, and the often-neglected muscles in your face. When you've finished the procedure from head to toe, take a few minutes to lie quietly and notice how your entire body feels. Open your eyes slowly, and stretch before resuming your daily routine.

WORRY-FREE DINING

Don't bring your worries to the dinner table—help keep them away with worry-doll napkin rings you make yourself! Take the cardboard tube from a paper towel roll, and cut it into two-inch-wide "mini-tubes." Wrap them in colorful fabric, or paint colorful designs on the rolls and let them dry. Finally, glue dolls onto the rings, and insert cloth napkins.

Try New Things

Many worrywarts shy away from trying new things because they are anxious about the unknown. But in actuality, new experiences can give you the confidence to let go of your worries. When you overcome your fears and obstacles, you feel more capable of facing new challenges.

"Thrill-seeking" activities such as bungee jumping or hang-gliding can not only boost your confidence, but also make you realize how insignificant your concerns are when faced with dangers that are real and tangible. But you don't need to start out with such overwhelming adventures—simply putting yourself in an unfamiliar situation is enough. So enroll in that photography class you always meant to take, learn how to sing like an opera star, take a trip by yourself, or seek out new friends. Do something to shake up your daily routine. And don't forget to bring your worry dolls along for the ride!

If you fail at your new challenges, you should still feel good about yourself for having taken risks instead of hiding under a rock and letting life pass you by. If things don't go as planned, get up, dust off, and try something else.

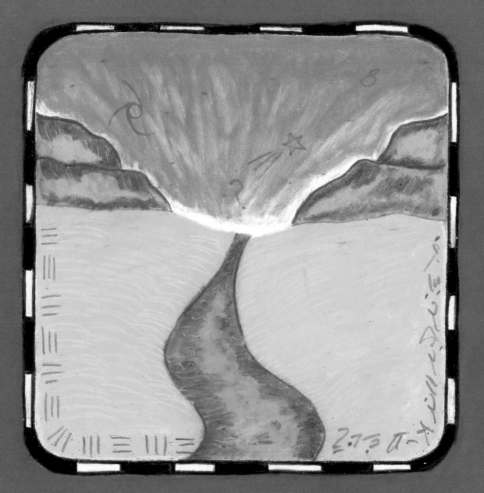

Focus on the Present

Label your worries! This exercise

can be accomplished either in your

head or in your worry journal.

The idea is to get to the root of your worries by labeling them, and thus see them for what they really are. Pay close attention to your thought process, and when a worry enters your mind, try to figure out if it comes from the past, present, or future. Ruminating on an argument you had with your sister several months ago should be labeled "past." Paying this month's bills might be considered "present," and fears that start out "What if…" should be categorized as "future" concerns. Now imagine writing the "past," "present," or "future" label on each of your worries with a big felt-tipped marker (or actually do so in your worry journal).

Compartmentalizing your fears chronologically can help you focus on your present worries instead of wasting precious energy on events that have already happened or ones that may never come to pass. Focusing on the present can help you feel more powerful in handling your problems; it's hard to have control over past events unless you have a secret for traveling back in time. It's also difficult to have control

over future situations, unless you have a crystal ball and can predict all of the hidden variables that might come into play.

Next try to label each present worry for what it really is. If you're throwing a party and are worried that no one will show up, you might give that worry the label "fear of rejection." If you're afraid you did a bad job on a work project, you might label the worry "insecurity" or "perfection-ism." If you're afraid of getting into a car accident, it might be an issue about feeling out of control. You might write "fear of physical harm." It's easier to combat worry if you discover its source and come to understand what it's really about.

ON YOUR MARK

You don't have to worry about losing your place in a book when you have your own special bookmark. Cut a strip of colorful construction paper into a six-by-two-inch strip. Have the paper laminated at a copy store. You could use a strip of cloth or ribbon in place of the paper. Next glue a worry doll at the head of the strip so the tiny figure will stick out of the top of a book when you want to save your spot. Now when you're trying to wind down after a hard day with a good novel, you'll have a little extra assistance.

Take Baby Steps

Many worriers build up a situation in their minds to such a degree that it seems insurmountable. To conquer this phenomenon, you need to break the problem into small pieces you can digest. One way to do this is to draw a picture of stairs. At the top of the steps, write your perfect resolution to the problem. For example, if you're planning to move and it seems overwhelming, jot down "all moved in."

Next, drop to the bottom step, and write underneath it the first action you need to take to get you started toward the end goal. Make sure the first step is an easy one, such as collecting boxes for packing. Now, populate the rest of the stairs with other small steps you'll need to take. The second step might be reserving a moving van. Other steps could include setting up the utilities at your new home, packing, or holding a garage sale. You'll realize that if you take "baby steps" toward your goal, it's much easier than trying to jump the whole staircase at once.

A similar exercise gives you permission to worry about only one thing at a time. Take a pen and a piece of paper, and write out a personal contract. If you have a big project looming, set realistic goals you'd like to meet. For example, jot down the dates

> *"Let our advance worrying become advance thinking and planning."* —Sir Winston Churchill

by which you'd like to have the research, outline, rough draft, and final copy done (giving yourself a buffer in case things don't go as planned). Concentrate only on the one activity with the upcoming deadline. If you are at the research stage, for example, worry only about that deadline, not about finishing the final draft.

Next set a guideline for how much time you're allowed to focus on the issue each day. For example, set the goal that you'll work on the project for three hours per day, but for the rest of the day you won't be allowed to think about it at all. This may seem like a strange thing to do, but worrywarts often

need to give themselves permission not to worry.

You may also want to include other rules in the contract. For example, say that the rough draft has to be really rough, and don't allow yourself to use correct grammar or get neurotic about making it perfect. Finally, sign your name at the bottom of the contract so you can't go back on your word. You'll probably discover that having all the conditions written down on paper will make the project or issue at hand easier to manage.

Spring Cleaning

Many people engage in the yearly ritual of spring cleaning—unearthing the rags and cleaning supplies and removing the dust and grime from the smallest of crevices. They often toss out what they no longer need in the process. Why not take the time to "spring clean" your mind and spirit by throwing out emotional baggage that no longer serves you well? Wipe your mind clean of the unhealthy habits that are holding you back.

First, you must identify the negative qualities that need to be tossed. Excessive worrying should be the first to go. Second, get rid of the causes of the worries—mentally burn your insecurities, trade in your control-freak ways for a more carefree attitude, and take your perfectionism to the junkyard. Now, dig out your great qualities that need to be dusted off and restored to their full potential.

Since we're so busy living our lives, we frequently forget to take stock of what is helpful and harmful in our environment. Sit down and make a list of the activities and people that play an active role in your life. This could

"The crisis of today is the joke of tomorrow." —H. G. Wells, British writer

include work, hobbies, school, errands, chores, entertainment, friends, coworkers, or family members. Put a plus (+) symbol next to each of the people and activities that give you energy, and a minus (-) sign next to those that drain it. If the positive and negative are fairly balanced, you can use an equal (=) sign instead.

Take a good, hard look at the people with minus signs next to them. It may be difficult to do, but you may need to reduce involvement or sever contact with those people who tend to "hoover up" your energy. Next, take a peek at the activities. If you have a negative sign next to your job, it

may be time to seek a career change. Are there chores or errands you find particularly laborious? Maybe you can swap chores with your spouse or a friend—or even hire somebody to take on these tedious tasks.

Not all of your spring cleaning needs to be so abstract. You may actually find that cleaning your house from top to bottom can be quite therapeutic. It also feels great to throw out clutter that's been bogging you down and to purge mementos from less enjoyable times.

Use Your Imagination

Discover how you can use your imagination to combat worry and develop a positive attitude!

First you'll need to find a quiet spot to lie down where you won't be interrupted. Get comfortable, close your eyes and release any tensions you've been holding in your body—just let your muscles relax. Next picture the subject of your worry. For example, if you have a daunting project, visualize yourself sitting down and working on it. Picture your office, recreating all the details of your surroundings in your mind—including sights, sounds, and smells. It's normal for you to feel tense and anxious during this part of the exercise.

Now walk yourself through the steps needed to complete the task. Imagine the best possible outcome—that you've finished the project earlier than expected, and your boss likes it so much she gives you a promotion. Concentrate on how good it feels to exceed your expectations.

Imagining your task in its full context—the benefits of success and the minor setbacks of failure—can limit its negative impact on your psyche. Meanwhile, visualizing the perfect outcome may help you

find the confidence to complete the task instead of worrying about it. The positive scenario gives you something for which to strive. It can also work a little bit like "wish fulfillment"—the powerful subconscious pursuit of your heart's desire—possibly because it gives you the chance to figure out exactly what you really want and what you really need.

"...visualizing the perfect outcome may help you find the confidence to complete the task..."

You can also use your imagination for those times when you need to take a mental vacation from your worries. Instead of picturing the object of your anxiety, close your eyes and imagine you are somewhere calm and peaceful. It could be a mountaintop, a meadow, or a particular spot where you feel serene. Next, think about what each of your senses would be experiencing in this place. Imagine the sounds of the birds, the wind blowing through the trees, or a babbling brook. Then take a deep breath and smell the crisp fresh air. *Guided imagery* exercises such as these have been found to reduce tension, and even to lower blood pressure under stressful conditions.

Positively Positive

Make a list of all your positive qualities and the major accomplishments in your life. Include events that may have started out badly but ended up working out for the best. How will this list stop you from fretting? It will show you that not everything turns out negatively—in fact, things often turn out much better than you expected. Worrywarts often think the worst is bound to come true—this list will prove that this perspective is distorted.

Writing down your positive attributes combats the self-doubter in you, diminishing the feelings that you won't be able to handle a situation the right way. Giving your self-esteem a boost can help you feel that you can competently and confidently accomplish what you need to do.

Write down the fact that you finished college, that you're a great parent or friend, that you have a terrific green thumb, or that your partner dumped you but you ended up in a much better relationship. If you're having difficulty picking out your good points, invite a group of supportive friends to come over, and share what you like most about each other. Now, whenever your inner voices tell you that you aren't good enough, take out this list, and read about the special, amazing person you are!

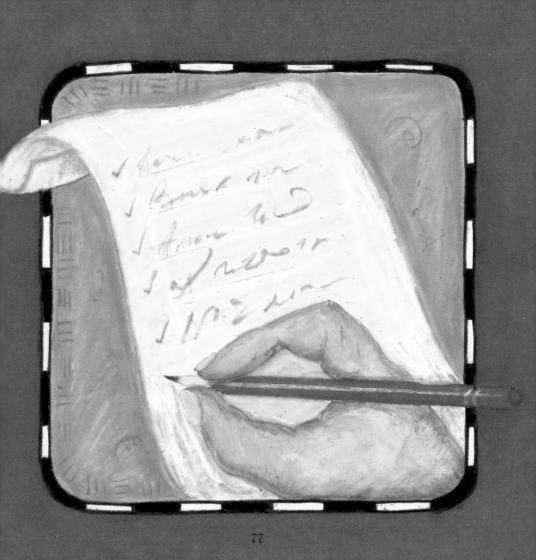

Mellowing Music

FA LA LA

Listening to music can put you in an altered, more serene frame of mind. Some like to be consoled by the blues (because "misery loves company"), others like the calming effects of classical or jazz, while still others prefer the angst-releasing benefits of heavy metal. Make a mix tape or CD of your favorite songs that help you to relax. Sing along to it while stuck in traffic, or pop it in your stereo and dance away your worries.

Looking for new songs to help diminish your worrywart tendencies? Bobby McFerrin's "Don't Worry, Be Happy" won a Grammy —probably because so many people are looking to learn how to do just that. Everybody loved *The Lion King's* hit, "Hakuna Matata," which means "no worries," in case you didn't already know. It happens to be sung by a fuzzy meerkat and a wild boar, which adds to its feel-good charm. If you like reggae, the chorus of Bob Marley's "Three Little Birds" says, "Don't worry 'bout a thing, 'cause every little thing's gonna be all right"—and isn't that what we all need to hear? Finally, Louis Armstrong's "What a Wonderful World" just helps us to remember the simple but beautiful things life has to offer.

Writing your own song lyrics or music is another great way to

release overwhelming worries. If the words just aren't coming to you, try getting a bongo drum and beating out the rhythms of your frustrations.

SECRET PALS

Do you have friends, coworkers, or a spouse who frequently seem to be stressed out? Try hiding the dolls around their houses or offices as pleasant reminders to relax. If you're feeling especially sneaky, the figures can be slipped easily into pockets or purses to combat tension on the go. People appreciate friends looking out for them, and almost everybody likes surprises, too. If your worrywarts already know how the dolls work, they will appreciate the thoughtfulness behind this gift. If they don't know the power of the dolls, they will at least be intrigued, and perhaps distracted from their concerns. You can let the dolls pique their curiosity—telling them later about the special legend.

Letting Go Rituals

Invent rituals designed to symbolically release your anxieties. One technique is to cut out small pieces of paper, and write your troubles on them. Then roll up the tiny notes and put them in helium balloons. Take the balloons outside to release them. Wave goodbye as your worries drift off.

Another method for exorcising anxieties is to host a "Bonfire of Burdens." Invite friends over for tea, and have everyone jot down their worries on a sheet of paper. At the end of the evening, toss the lists into the fireplace. If you have more time, gather up your troops and go on a camping trip. This way, you can build a real bonfire for burning your troubles.

For some letting-go rituals you'll need only your imagination. Try blowing bubbles, and pretending your worries are inside each one as they float away. Or pop the bubbles to put an end to the worry once and for all. Because rituals can be very personal, you may need to try different ones to find out which ones work best to reduce your anxiety level.

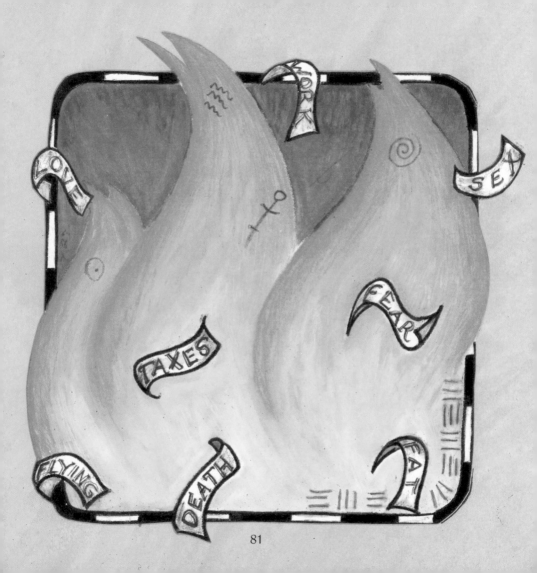

TAKE IT TO THE TOP

Keep your worry dolls close to where worry starts—your head! Visit a craft store, and buy a barrette clasp and colorful embroidery thread. Wind the thread around the clasp until it's completely covered. Next, glue the worry dolls onto the hairpiece. Now every time you start to fret, just reach on top of your noggin and remember that tiny friends are watching over you!

If you can't find a barrette clasp, you can use the Guatemalan figures to decorate any store-bought barrette, hair elastic, or ornamental chopsticks. For men, the dolls can be used for a unique tie clasp, an original set of cuff links, or for a special watchband.

One of the best techniques for combating worry is actually one of the easiest—just breathe! You will find that practicing *deep relaxation* methods, such as abdominal breathing, for twenty to thirty minutes each day will reduce generalized anxiety and prevent stress from accumulating. Under duress, breathing often becomes rapid and shallow, and begins in the chest. When relaxed, you'll breath more deeply, from your diaphragm in your abdominal area. Deep breathing increases the supply of oxygen to the brain and stimulates the parasympathetic nervous system, which promotes a state of calmness. Breathing techniques also can help you feel more connected to your body, so you aren't concentrating solely on

eath

the negative thoughts running amok in your brain.

To practice abdominal breathing, try to find a quiet spot where you won't be disturbed. Lie flat on your back, and place one hand on your chest and the other on your abdomen, right above your bellybutton. Close your eyes, and release any tension you've been holding in your muscles. Next inhale slowly and deeply through your nose. If you are breathing from your diaphragm, your abdomen should rise while your chest remains still. When you've taken in a full breath, pause for a moment and then slowly exhale through your nostrils.

Try to keep your breathing smooth and regular. To do this, try counting slowly to three while inhaling, and again counting slowly to three while letting the air out. For a more meditative technique, you could also try counting each exhalation: inhale, pause for a moment, then count "one" as you exhale. Continue counting each time you exhale, up to the number ten, and then repeat two more times.

If you aren't in a situation where you can take the time to lie in a quiet spot, you can still practice your abdominal breathing. That's probably the best part of this tension-busting practice—you can do it anywhere you feel stress: in a meeting, on the bus, or in the dentist's chair!

"Live in each season as it passes; breathe the air, drink the drink, taste the fruit, and resign yourself to the influences of each."

—*Henry David Thoreau*

When you're feeling like you can't handle the stresses in your life, take the time to pamper yourself. When you're all wound up, unwind with a low-budget spa night in your own home. Indulgences might include a bubble bath with candles, soothing music, or chocolate treats. You might follow your soak with a facial and pedicure.

Or blow off steam by dancing, participating in sports, or engaging in stimulating video games. Reduce tension with activities like reading, meditation, playing with pets, blowing bubbles, or singing at the top of your lungs. Experiment to find out what really soothes your soul and eases you into a serene frame of mind.

Be your own Best Friend

Do you often find yourself saying, "I am such an idiot!" or "I never do anything right"? When you stop to think about it, do the things you tell yourself when worrying seem just a bit extreme? You could be blowing tiny failures out of proportion while downplaying positive achievements.

Watch what you're telling yourself. Use your worry journal to write down criticisms verbatim, and see if they make any sense. Your phrasing may be more significant than you realize. If you constantly tell yourself that you're no good, you might start believing your self-characterization. Go a little easier on yourself, and transform the voice in your head from a royal nag into your closest ally.

Stop to think whether you might be overreacting. Is it really the end of the world if you overslept and missed the bus? Does this automatically mean you always miss appointments or earn you the title "Super Sloth"? You might have done poorly on a test or failed to perform up to your usual high standards on a particular project. But there could have been extenuating circumstances: it could have been a rough week, or maybe it was a difficult test that nobody did well on. You might have also set yourself unreasonable expectations.

One failure does not mean that you will always fail. Ask yourself if you are being reasonable with your self-assessments. Take a look at the dolls when you are beating yourself up over something. Voice fears to them instead of talking inside your head. Their blank looks and smiles can be quite appropriate—if they could talk, they might ask, "Hey, what's the big deal?"

Chances are, the self-inflicted punishment you are doling out does not fit the crime of such minor setbacks. Watch out when your inner voice uses words such as "never" and "always." Play down those perfectionist impulses. Everybody fails sometimes. It's important to realize that even if you flub in one area of your life you are often succeeding at the same time on something else.

Allow yourself to acknowledge your accomplishments, and keep perspective on your slip-ups.

One particularly effective way to monitor what you're telling yourself is to think what you would tell a friend under similar circumstances. If your friend told you that she felt like a jerk for ending a relationship, you'd be unlikely to say, "You're right, you really are a jerk!" Instead, you would probably tell her that she was being too hard on herself, or point out that she wouldn't have given up if something weren't seriously wrong with the relationship. Your own psyche deserves the same fair and balanced treatment. Act toward yourself as you would act toward others, and you'll find a friend in your inner voice.

Mellow Out

If modern living is causing you to stress, try some age-old remedies to restore balance, harmony, and a sense of well-being. Meditation, acupuncture, and acupressure have been used for thousands of years to promote health and alleviate mental and physical strain.

Meditation is a popular method for relaxing and restoring used in both the East and the West. In meditation, you sit still and focus your mind repeatedly and thoroughly on one thing, whether it's a word, an image, a concept, or simply your breathing. This mental focus helps to still the thinking process—and the worries spinning around in your brain. Meditation has been shown to increase self-esteem, decrease anxiety and depression, and lead to better overall health.

Acupuncture and acupressure are healing techniques designed to open the constricted channels by putting pressure on specific areas. According to Eastern wisdom, poor health is a result of blocked internal energy, and worrying is a classic way to obstruct the flow.

While it's understandable to be afraid of the needles used in acupuncture, most people barely feel a thing. If you can't shake your apprehension, try acupressure—it involves only the exertion of pressure on your body's "pressure points," and has effects similar to those of acupuncture. The end result of either practice is a feeling of serenity and well-being.

WRAP WORRIES AWAY

Do you want to do something special for a friend who is drowning in a pool of stress? Assemble a customized antiworry package that includes a worry stone, a blank worry journal, lavender bath salts (the smell of lavender is said to promote relaxation), and a soothing mix tape. Wrap the gift in cheerful paper and decorate the package with the playful worry dolls. You can tape the dolls onto the paper, or glue them to the ribbon. Voilà! You have created a "worry-free" masterpiece.

Sound Mind

Consider studying a martial art or meditative discipline like yoga or tai chi. In these practices, the emphasis on physical awareness and a centered mind can equip you to deal with the worries you face every day.

Yoga is an East Indian practice that combines breathing techniques and a variety of stretches, or "poses." Tai chi is a slow Chinese martial art that involves precise sets of movements called *forms*. Both practices were developed to stimulate the circulation of internal energy, while at the same

 *Body*

time focusing your mind on your body in a meditative way. The end result is similar: enhanced balance and a sense of physical comfort and power, as well as a tranquil and grounded mental state.

While yoga and tai chi focus on stretching positions and slow, meditative motions, martial arts like tae kwon do, aikido, or karate are composed of more intense physical exercises. Some people shy away from the aggressive elements of these activities, but many enjoy the unique mental, physical, and spiritual challenges they present. You might feel empowered by joining a class—the energy you feel when the group shouts in unison or practices synchronized forms can be exhilarating. (Plus, how often do you get to let loose a yell in regular life?) You might also like the self-control you acquire while practicing motions on your own.

Martial arts cleanse the mind by allowing it to focus on the body—there is no room for anxiety in a focused mind. The antiworry benefits associated with being able to defend yourself and carry yourself with confidence are also quite rewarding.

Power in Numbers

Although the magic number of worry dolls for your pillowcase is six, you might find the need to make more of your own, especially if you plan to use them in some of the craft projects mentioned in this book. Spending time making dolls might even distract you from your worries, or give you time to focus your thoughts. If you have children, tell them the legend and let them join in. They will enjoy being a part of this process, and might like the idea of the mysterious tale.

There are several ways to make worry dolls. In Guatemala, children use whatever scrap materials are available. Toothpicks, small strips of thin cardboard, or the wire twist-ties that come with garbage bags can be used to form the backbones of the dolls. For larger dolls (which are easier for small children to make), you can use old wooden clothespins for the bodies (the kinds without metal springs).

If you choose to make the dolls from wire twist-ties, fold one in half for the head, torso, and legs (in this case the head would be at the fold). Then use another wire—perhaps doubled-up—to make the arms. This method creates dolls about the right size to use on small craft projects like the journal, bookmark, and frames suggested in this book. For larger projects, like the wreaths, you might make the dolls from a bigger base, perhaps by using the clothespin technique. Keep in mind that a small bit of glue can help hold the parts in place.

Finish forming the body, then wind colorful embroidery floss or yarn around it, starting at the legs and moving up the torso. Clothe the dolls with tiny pieces of fabric. Faces can be drawn in at the end on skin-colored thread or cardboard left sticking out at the top.

Experiment! Worry-doll hair is often made with glue and sand. For variety, you could try glitter-and-glue hairdos. Worries come in many forms; your dolls can, too. Personalize your worry dolls and make them suit your fancy. Let them help you lose your cares!

Suggested Reading

A WORRYWART'S READING LIST

Breton, Sue. *Don't Panic: A Guide to Overcoming Panic Attacks.* New York: Facts on File, 1986.

Bruno, Frank. *Stop Worrying: Understand Your Anxiety— and Banish It Forever!* New York: Simon and Schuster Macmillan Inc., 1997.

Carlson, Richard. *Don't Sweat the Small Stuff... and It's All Small Stuff.* New York: Hyperion, 1997.

Carnegie, Dale. *How to Stop Worrying and Start Living.* Revised Edition. New York: Simon and Schuster, 1984.

Gordon, Lynn, and Jessica Hurley. *52 Relaxing Rituals.* San Francisco: Chronicle Books,1996.

Hart, Carol. *Secrets of Serotonin.* New York: St. Martin's Press, 1996.

Harvey, John R. *Total Relaxation: Healing Practices for Body, Mind & Spirit.* New York: Kodansha America Inc., 1998.

Potter, Beverley. *The Worrywart's Companion: Twenty-One Ways to Soothe Yourself and Worry Smart.* Berkeley, CA: Wildcat Canyon Press, 1997.

Wilson, R. Reid. *Don't Panic: Taking Control of Anxiety Attacks.* New York: Harper & Row, 1986.

GUATEMALAN / WORRY DOLL READING LIST

Asturias, Miguel Angel, and Frances Partridge (translator). *The President.* Reprint Edition. Prospect Heights, IL: Waveland Press, 1997.

Buffett, Jimmy. *Trouble Dolls.* (Juvenile Literature.) San Diego: Harcourt Brace Jovanovich, 1991.

Harbury, Jennifer. *Bridge of Courage: Life Stories of the Guatemalan Compañeros and Compañeras.* Monroe, ME: Common Courage Press, 1995.

Menchu, Rigoberta. *I, Rigoberta Menchu: An Indian Woman in Guatemala.* London: Verso, 1984.

Regan, Dian. *Curse of the Trouble Dolls.* (Juvenile Literature.) New York: H. Holt, 1992.

Schevill, Margot Blum. *Maya Textiles of Guatemala.* Austin, TX: University of Texas Press, 1993.

Schlesinger, Stephen C., et al. *Bitter Fruit: The Story of the American Coup in Guatemala.* Expanded Edition. Cambridge, MA: Harvard University Press, 1999.

Simon, Jean-Marie. *Guatemala: Eternal Spring Eternal Tyranny.* New York: W.W. Norton & Company Inc., 1987.

Temko, Florence. *Traditional Crafts from Mexico and Central America.* (Juvenile Crafts.) Minneapolis, MN: Lerner Publications, 1996.

About the Author

JESSICA HURLEY has coauthored (with Lynn Gordon) a series of popular activity cards, with titles including *52 Relaxing Rituals*, *52 Ways to Stay Young at Heart*, and *52 Party Activities for Grown-ups*. Born on April Fool's Day 1970 in Berkeley, California, Jessica was raised on a hippie commune, where she lived in a subterranean dwelling called the "Hole." Among other adventures, she has traveled with a rock band, worked for a toy company, and learned to spin fire. She wrote a portion of this book while in India, in the community of the Dalai Lama and the Tibetan government-in-exile. Jessica currently works for Oxygen Media as a producer for ThriveOnline, a Webby Award–winning Web site on healthy living. She lives in San Francisco, California.

About the Illustrator

PADDY BRUCE is a designer, illustrator, and fine artist who has long been influenced by Central American art styles. Her artwork is featured in *Milagros: A Book of Miracles* and various other publications. Paddy has studied abroad at the London School of Design and Dressmaking in London, England; at the Universidad de las Americas in Mexico City, Mexico; and at the famed Instituto Allende de Arte in San Miguel Allende, Mexico. A former teacher of art and art history, she currently runs her own design-and-illustration business, Art & Soul. She lives in Bellingham, Washington.